Twenty to Make

Modern Needlepoint

Jayne Schofield

Search Press

First published in 2016

Search Press Limited
Wellwood, North Farm Road,
Tunbridge Wells, Kent TN2 3DR

Text copyright © Jayne Schofield 2016

Photographs by Paul Bricknell at
Search Press Studios

Photographs and design copyright
© Search Press Ltd 2016

Print ISBN: 978-1-78221-226-3
ebook ISBN: 978-1-78126-268-9

Suppliers
If you have difficulty in obtaining any of the
materials and equipment mentioned in this book,
then please visit the Search Press website for
details of suppliers: www.searchpress.com

Printed in China

Dedication

*To my husband Doug and son Ben, for the support
they gave me during the time that I worked on
the designs for this book.*

Contents

Introduction 4

Stitching instructions 6

Apple 8

Baby Boy 10

Regatta 12

Beach Huts 14

Butterfly 16

Cat 18

Circles 20

Daisies 22

Dutch Tile 24

Three Fish 26

Nesting Hen 28

Town House 30

Jug and Flower 32

Owl 34

Baby Girl 36

Reindeer 38

Sheep 40

Snowman 42

Tulips 44

Folk House 46

Introduction

I am delighted to introduce to you my first needlepoint book. The designs within these pages are a reflection of many of the things that I love, including nature, flowers, home and family. The colours used in my designs are influenced by those found within my garden, from the rich pinks of my fuchsias to the vibrant greens of the foliage; I like to draw from nature's palette.

My design process usually begins with a series of simple line drawings around the chosen theme, and from these I select elements I feel will work together. I then cut them out and play around with size and composition until I feel that I have a working design. I spend a long time choosing the colour palette, mixing different wools together until I feel that I have the correct sentiment. I then begin to build the final artwork.

All of the designs within this book would look perfect framed, but there are other ideas that you can try. By adding a fabric border to your piece you could turn it into a small pillow or wall hanging. Try adding a decorative button in each corner for extra interest. Your finished needlepoint could also be used as the focal point for a place mat or tote bag. There are so many creative ideas that you could explore.

I hope you enjoy stitching the designs within this book and that it inspires you to go on to explore the art of needlepoint in the future.

Stitching instructions

Materials

The needlepoint designs in this book were all stitched using 10 hole per inch (2.5cm) white interlock canvas. The canvas used for needlepoint can be quite stiff to handle and for larger projects it is advisable to attach your canvas to a frame. This makes handling a lot easier and avoids the shape of your work from distorting due to the stitching tension. However, for smaller projects, such as those within this book, a frame is not needed. It is a good idea to bind the edges of your canvas with masking tape before you start, to avoid your wool from snagging on the sides when stitching.

I have used Anchor tapestry wool throughout and the reference numbers in the colour keys refer to this brand of wool. However, there are plenty of other brands of tapestry wool available, which carry a wide range of bright colours that would be suitable for these projects. You will need a size 18 tapestry needle. It has a large eye, which makes it easy to thread the wool and a blunt end to make it easier to pass through the holes in the canvas.

Getting started

You should always start your stitching from the centre outwards. This will ensure that you fit the whole design on your measured piece of canvas. Locate the centre stitch of your graph by following the arrows on each side, top and bottom. Mark this centre stitch and start your piece from here.

When starting a new colour, leave a 2.5cm (1in) length of thread at the back of your work and then, while working your first row of stitches, catch this thread into the back of them to secure it in place. This is an alternative to using a knot, which can make the front of your work look a little lumpy. All the needlepoint designs in this book are worked using half-cross tent stitch (see opposite), which is a slanted stitch.

Reading the charts

Each single square on the chart represents one half-cross tent stitch. The symbol in that square represents the colour to be used, which is specified in the key.

Finishing your work

When ending a colour, run a 2.5cm (1in) length of wool through the stitches at the back of your work to secure and snip off.

How to work half-cross tent stitch

As the name implies, this method involves creating a slanted stitch (half a cross stitch) worked diagonally. It does not matter in which direction the stitches slant as long as they all slant in the same direction. Work in rows alternately from left to right and then right to left, counting the squares and following the colour key. Each square on the graph is one slanted stitch (see right).

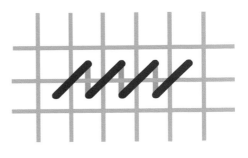

Symmetrical patterns

It is useful to bear in mind that when you are working symmetrical patterns that have diagonals, they will not look exactly the same on both sides because the stitches are worked from bottom left to top right. So, if you look at the cat's ears (right), for example, you will see that the left ear produces a ragged edge, while the right ear gives a straight edge. Similarly, with the whiskers, the right diagonal whisker is ragged, while the left diagonal whisker is straight. This is one of the quirky charms of needlepoint and adds to the appeal of hand-stitched work.

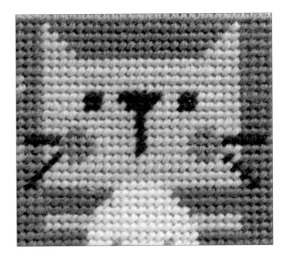

Blocking

When stitching needlepoint, the tension of the stitches makes the canvas skew. Because all the stitches lie in the same direction, it means that the wool is pulled constantly in that direction, causing the canvas to distort. The easiest way to prevent this is by using a tapestry frame. This holds the work tight while you are stitching and keeps the canvas square. If you choose not to use a tapestry frame, or your work is too small for a frame, then it will need blocking.

To do this, you will need a blocking board (or a flat piece of wood), some tacks and a water spray bottle. Mark out a grid on the wood to help you square up your work when blocking.

1 Remove any masking tape from around the edges of your canvas. Lightly dampen the work using a spray bottle and clean, tepid water.

2 Allow 10 minutes for the water to soften the wool fibres, then carefully stretch and tug the canvas to reshape.

3 Using the blocking board or flat piece of wood, tack the corners of the canvas down, making sure that they are all at right angles to each other. Tack down each side of the canvas in turn, making sure that you pull the damp canvas into shape to make each edge straight.

4 Allow the canvas to dry thoroughly before removing all the tacks.

Apple

Colour key:

•	White (8000)	↓	Bright blue (8804)
∖	Pale yellow (8016)	✳	Fuchsia pink (8454)
•∴	Lime green (9152)	╱	Purple (8588)
4	Rose pink (8486)	■	Red (8440)
∧	Bright orange (8140)	O	Denim blue (8644)

Stitching notes:

Stitch count: 48 x 48.

Design area: 12.2 x 12.2 cm (4¾ x 4¾ in) at 10 sts per 2.5 cm (1 in).

8

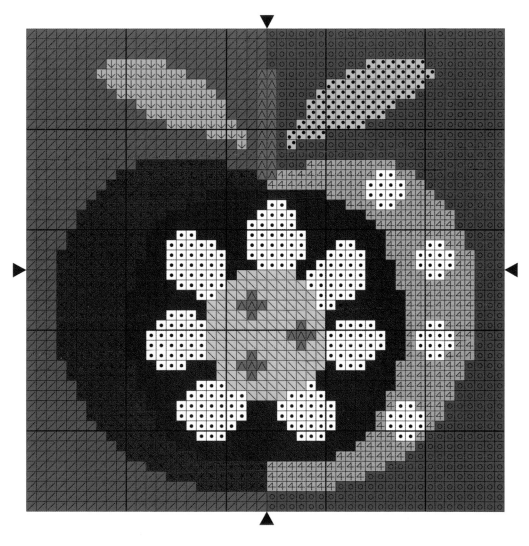

Baby Boy

Colour key:

 White (8000)

 Denim blue (8644)

⊙ Beige (9382)

◹ Lilac (8586)

◲ Bright blue (8804)

✳ Lavender (8606)

⇐ Petrol blue (8806)

4 Green (9172)

Stitching notes:

Stitch count: 40 x 45.

Design area: 10.2 x 11.4 cm (4 x 4½ in) at 10 sts per 2.5 cm (1 in).

10

11

Regatta

Colour key:

 White (8000)

• Pale blue (8802)

○ Lavender (8606)

✳ Spring blue (8686)

 Red (8440)

╱ Bright blue (8804)

▼ Denim blue (8644)

⊠ Navy (8738)

Stitching Notes:

Stitch count: 57 x 39.

Design area: 14.5 x 9.9 cm (5¾ x 3⅞ in) at 10 sts per 2.5 cm (1 in).

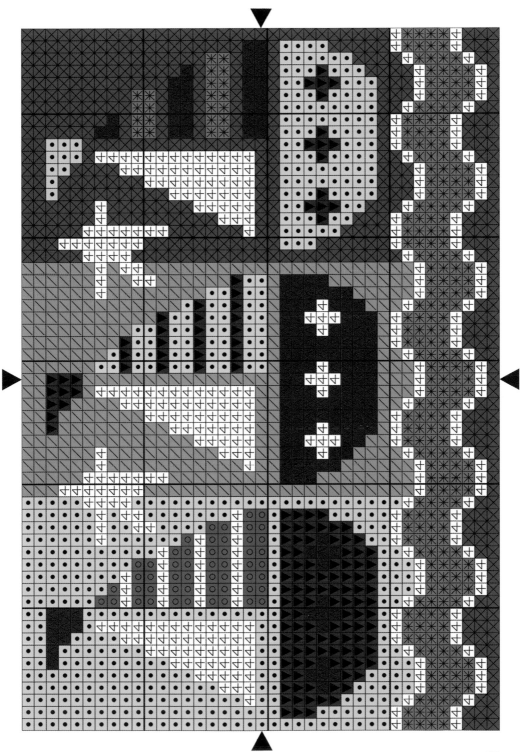

Beach Huts

Colour key:

• White (8000)		/ Lavender (8606)
Λ Pale yellow (8016)		Fuchsia pink (8454)
↑ Lime green (9152)		◉ Denim blue (8644)
✳ Bright blue (8804)		Red (8440)
♡ Bright orange (8140)		

Stitching notes:

Stitch count: 47 x 36.

Design area: 11.9 x 9.1 cm (4¾ x 3⁹⁄₁₆ in) at 10 sts per 2.5 cm (1 in).

Butterfly

Colour key:

•	White (8000)	✳	Orange (8136)
○	Light pink (8482)	4	Yellow (8038)
╱	Rose pink (8486)	⊠	Sage green (9094)
■	Fuchsia pink (8454)	∴	Bright blue (8804)
♥	Lavender (8606)		

Stitching notes:

Stitch count: 48 x 48.

Design area: 12.2 x 12.2 cm (4¾ x 4¾ in) at 10 sts per 2.5 cm (1 in).

Cat

Colour key:

⬚ Pale sand (8034)		4 Lilac (8586)	
• Yellow (8038)		✕ Lavender (8606)	
V Bright orange (8140)		✳ Black (9796)	
○ Rose pink (8486)			

Stitching notes:

Stitch count: 45 x 45.

Design area: 11.4 x 11.4 cm (4½ x 4½ in) at 10 sts per 2.5 cm (1 in).

18

Circles

Colour key:

△	White (8000)	◥	Russet (8398)
◺	Pale sand (8034)	◩	Lavender (8606)
↓	Beige (9382)	→	Bright blue (8804)
◹	Pale yellow (8016)	∨	Lilac (8586)
●	Pink (8542)	○	Green (9172)
✳	Rose pink (8486)		

Stitching notes:

Stitch count: 53 x 52.

Design area: 13.5 x 13.2 cm (5¼ x 5¼ in) at 10 sts per 2.5 cm (1 in).

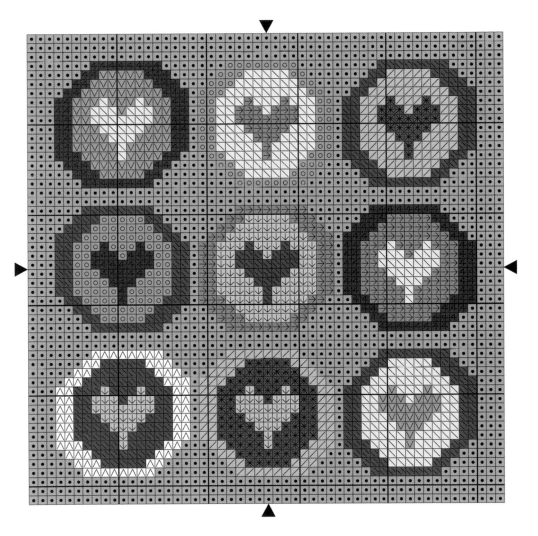

Daisies

Colour key:

•	Yellow (8038)	✕	Dark purple (8596)
╱	Orange (8136)	✳	Lavender (8606)
♡	Bright orange (8140)	4	Petrol blue (8806)
○	Rose pink (8486)	╲	Jade (8966)
▲	Fuchsia pink (8454)	↓	Lime (9152)
╱	Raspberry (8438)	→	Light grey (8622)

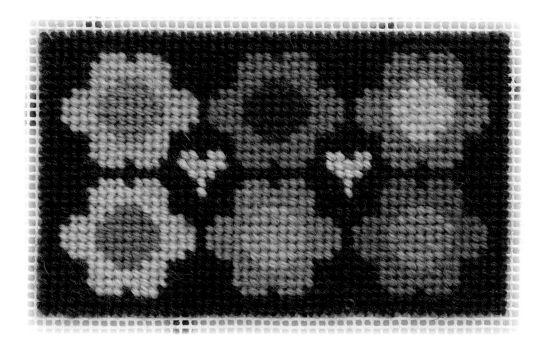

Stitching Notes:

Stitch count: 51 x 31.

Design area: 13 x 7.9 cm (5⅛ x 3⅛ in) at 10 sts per 2.5 cm (1 in).

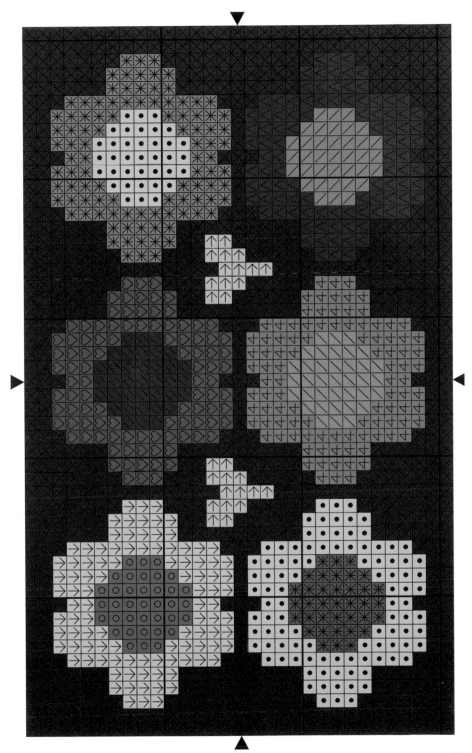

Dutch Tile

Colour key:

 Pale sand (8034)

Green (9172)

Jade (8966)

Bright blue (8804)

 Purple (8588)

Fuchsia pink (8454)

Rose pink (8486)

Light pink (8482)

Stitching Notes:

Stitch count: 49 x 47.

Design area: 12.4 x 11.9 cm (4⅛ x 4¾ in) at 10 sts per 2.5 cm (1 in).

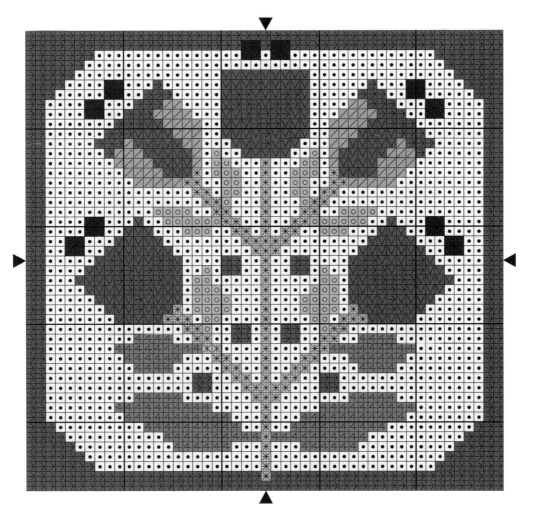

Three Fish

Colour key:

↓ White (8000)	╲ Green (9172)
○ Spring green (9192)	↑ Jade (8966)
4 Orange (8136)	• Bright blue (8804)
♡ Russet (8398)	╱ Lilac (8586)
✕ Rose pink (8486)	✳ Lavender (8606)
◣ Raspberry (8438)	⋀ Navy (8738)

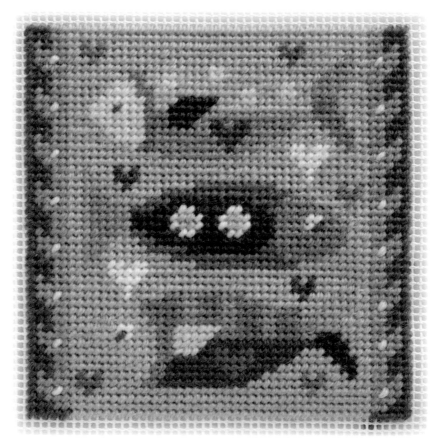

Stitching Notes:

Stitch count: 48 x 50.

Design area: 12.2 x 12.7 cm (4¾ x 5 in) at 10 sts per 2.5 cm (1 in).

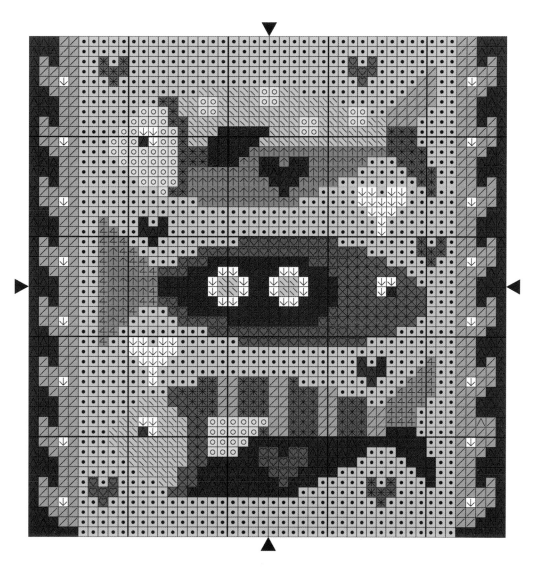

Nesting Hen

Colour key:

⦿	White (8000)	◼	Red (8440)
✳	Light grey (8622)	→	Bright blue (8804)
◩	Orange (8136)	◪	Lavender (8606)
⧄	Bright orange (8140)	◨	Navy (8738)

Stitching Notes:

Stitch count: 45 x 45.

Design area: 11.4 x 11.4 cm (4½ x 4½ in) at 10 sts per 2.5 cm (1 in).

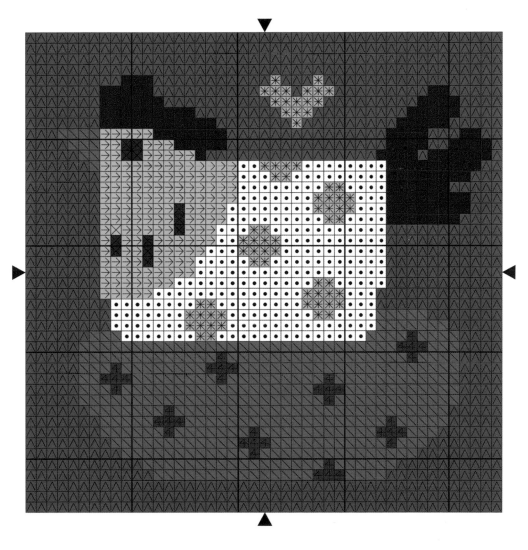

Colour key:

White (8000)		Lavender (8606)
Yellow (8038)		Lilac (8586)
Bright orange (8140)		Light grey (8622)
Sage green (9094)		Rose pink (8486)
Emerald (8984)		Russet (8398)
Bright blue (8804)		

Stitching Notes:

Stitch count: 49 x 49.

Design area: 12.4 x 12.4 cm (4⅞ x 4⅞ in) at 10 sts per 2.5 cm (1 in).

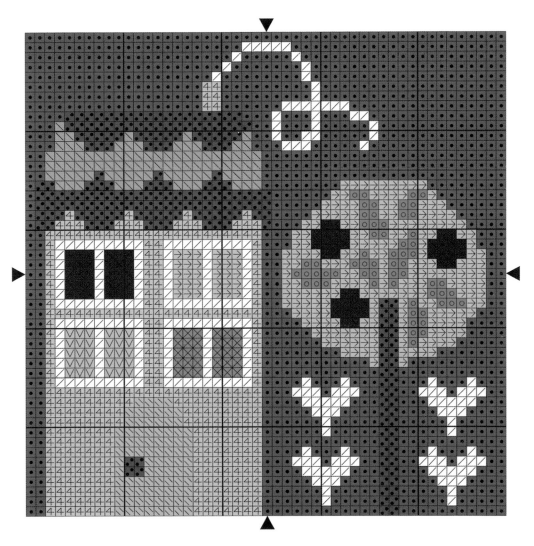

Jug and Flower

Colour key:

●	White (8000)	✳	Bright blue (8804)
╱	Yellow (8038)	4	Lavender (8606)
○	Pale blue (8802)	◹	Sugar pink (8484)

Stitching Notes:

Stitch count: 38 x 50.

Design area: 9.7 x 12.7 cm (3¾ x 5 in) at 10 sts per 2.5 cm (1 in).

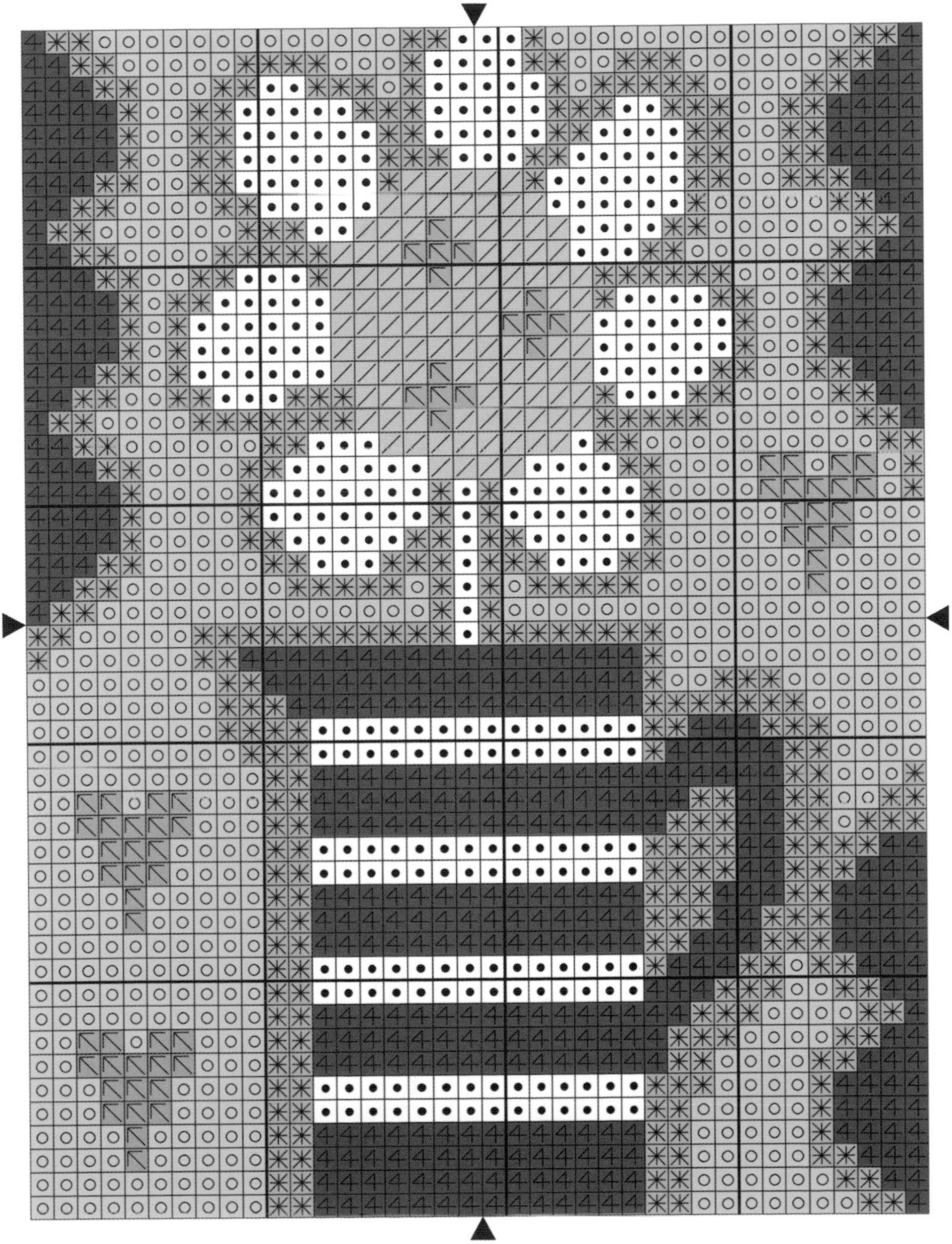

Colour key:

- ● White (8000)
- ╱ Pale yellow (8016)
- ○ Orange (8136)
- ╱\ Bright orange (8140)
- ■ Fuchsia pink (8454)
- ■ Raspberry (8438)
- ✳ Lavender (8606)
- ⊠ Lime green (9152)
- ← Jade (8966)
- ⫽ Bright blue (8804)
- ■ Brown (9452)

Stitching Notes:

Stitch count: 43 x 47.

Design area: 10.9 x 11.9 cm (4¼ x 4¾ in) at 10 sts per 2.5 cm (1 in).

Baby Girl

Colour key:

◩ White (8000)		↓ Heather (8524)	
● Sugar pink (8484)		◪ Bright blue (8804)	
◼ Fuchsia pink (8454)		✳ Purple (8588)	
◎ Russet (8398)		4 Yellow (8038)	

Stitching notes:

Stitch count: 40 x 45.

Design area: 10.2 x 11.4 cm (4 x 4½ in) at 10 sts per 2.5 cm (1 in).

36

Reindeer

Colour key:

 White (8000)

Light grey (8622)

Red (8440)

Black (9796)

Stitching Notes:

Stitch count: 39 x 53.

Design area: 9.9 x 13.5 cm (3⅞ x 5¼ in) at 10 sts per 2.5 cm (1 in).

Sheep

Colour key:

⊡	White (8000)
◩	Light grey (8622)
4	Bright blue (8804)
✳	Purple (8588)
→	Denim blue (8644)
◼	Navy (8738)
◉	Fuchsia pink (8454)
◼	Red (8440)

Stitching Notes:

Stitch count: 72 x 30.

Design area: 18.3 x 7.6 cm (7¼ x 3 in) at 10 sts per 2.5 cm (1 in).

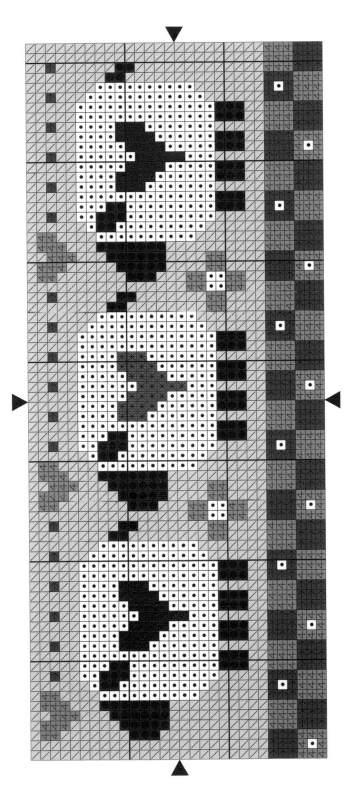

Snowman

Colour key:

⊡	White (8000)		⧄	Pale blue (8802)
◥	Sugar pink (8484)		４	Bright blue (8804)
▪	Red (8440)		←	Denim blue (8644)
✳	Bright orange (8140)		⊙	Purple (8588)
⊠	Sage green (9094)		▪	Black (9796)

Stitching Notes:

Stitch count: 44 x 52.

Design area: 11.2 x 13.2 cm (4⁷⁄₁₆ x 5¼ in) at 10 sts per 2.5 cm (1 in).

43

Tulips

Colour key:

	Pale sand (8034)		Lilac (8586)
	Orange (8136)		Bright blue (8804)
	Tangerine (8154)		Denim blue (8644)
	Rose pink (8486)		Lime green (9152)
	Fuchsia pink (8454)		Jade (8966)

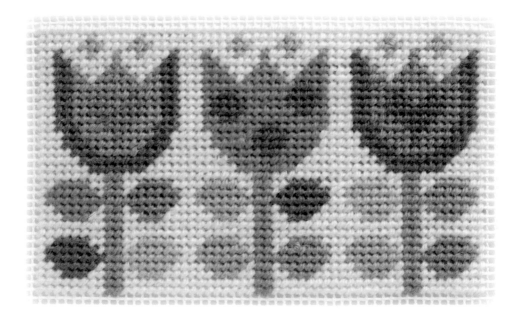

Stitching Notes:

Stitch count: 54 x 33.

Design area: 13.7 x 8.4 cm (5⅜ x 3¼ in) at 10 sts per 2.5 cm (1 in).

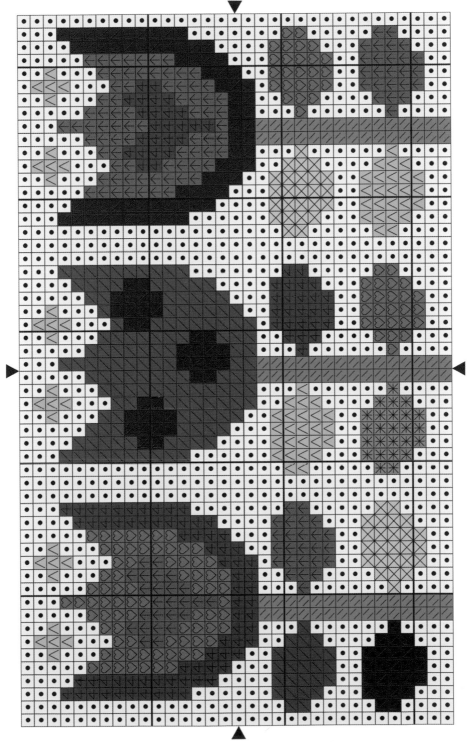

Folk House

Colour key:

-  White (8000)
- ∨ Green (9172)
- ╱ Dark green (9176)
- ■ Plum (8526)
- ○ Rose pink (8486)
- ✳ Lavender (8606)

Stitching Notes:

Stitch count: 51 x 39.

Design area: 13 x 9.9 cm (5⅛ x 3⅞ in) at 10 sts per 2.5 cm (1 in).

Publisher's Note

If you have enjoyed stitching these designs, then why not try something larger? Visit the author's website at: www.thestitchingshed.co.uk

Acknowledgements

I was delighted to be asked to produce this book and have thoroughly enjoyed putting it together. However, I could not have done it without the help, support and skill of the following people:

Thank you to my husband, Doug, for keeping me supplied with coffee and cake through the long hours and for being a fabulous needlepoint stitcher; my son, Ben, for your ability to keep me entertained throughout the whole process with your humour, wit and all-round loveliness; my mum and nana who inspired in me the love of needlework from a very early age; and to my grandad, who taught me about the joy of painting.

Thank you to all the people over the years who have bought my designs and supported me in my career as a needlecraft designer. Your support has enabled me to work in a job I love, and for that I am very grateful.